A CRISIS OF BEING

Sharon Thompson

A Crisis of Being

© 2023 Sharon Thompson

Published by Texianer Verlag
Johannesstraße 12
78609 Tuningen
Germany
www.texianer.com

for
The Hugh & Helene Schonfield
World Service Trust
www.schonfield.org
ISBN: 9798215064450

ABOUT THE AUTHOR

Sharon Thompson and her husband of sixty three years, Gordon, a retired dairy farmer, are the parents of six daughters (and now six sons-in-law) who have blessed them with twenty grandchildren and sixteen great-grandchildren. Her family is her greatest love and joy. Her hope is that this book will play a role in advancing a worldwide movement that will lead to a reclaimed world of love, peace, and justice for all people everywhere.

Contents

INTRODUCTION

I was a born non-believer. One of my earliest memories is deciding that Santa Claus did not really exist. Why? He was supposed to arrive in a sleigh pulled by flying reindeer. I knew that reindeer can't fly, therefore there had to be another reason that presents would appear under the Christmas tree. The next victim was the Tooth Fairy. I witnessed my Dad tossing my older sister's lost tooth into the goose mash. I then knew that he was the one who left a small amount of money in place of the tooth. The Easter Bunny didn't stand a chance. I had, early on, put God into the same category as Santa Claus, the Tooth Fairy, and the Easter Bunny.

Our family belonged to a large Congregational church in a nearby town and we attended on a regular basis. I hated Sunday School and church. I was too shy to make any friends in Sunday School and I questioned much of what I was hearing in the lessons. I recall being horrified upon learning that God chose to kill all of the first-born Egyptian children in the Passover story. What if I had been an Egyptian child and not one of God's Chosen People? It just didn't seem fair to me that he had favorites. Since I couldn't actually see God or hear him speak, then to my thinking, he did not exist.

Jesus wasn't as much of a problem. He seemed much nicer than God and seemed pretty much like an ordinary person. I didn't believe in any of the miracles he supposedly performed and did not believe that he had been resurrected. When people die, they stay dead. At my young age and forever after, I was wise enough to not let any of this be known to anyone, because religious beliefs seemed pretty important to most people.

The years passed. I dated the "boy next door" through most of high school and we were married in June after I graduated. I joined the small Lutheran church that generations of his family had attended and I became part of a close-knit Norwegian farming community. Sadly, the church and the community succumbed to "progress" and many of the former farms have been developed as housing projects. We have never met most of their occupants.

Getting back to my religious life: At twenty years of age I had an experience that convinced me that (1) God did exist, (2) he/she had a plan for humanity, and (3) I was expected to be a part of it. I had a toddler and a baby at the time and I helped in the barn for the evening milking. (My mother-in-law baby-sat while I was in the barn.) It would be many years before what was expected of me became at all clear. I assumed it had something to do with the church, and I became much more involved, including taking a teacher training class to teach a class called The Bethel Bible Series. It featured a picture with a short explanation of the essence of each lesson—a method I found very effective. I completed the course, but never taught because we were blessed with twin daughters shortly after completing the course and for good measure, we had a fifth daughter a little over a year later.

When the girls started Sunday School, I was recruited

to teach. I was assigned to the eighth grade class whose curriculum was the Old Testament. I wrote my own lessons using the text *Understanding the Old Testament* by Bernhard Anderson, a very competent scholar. I found using simple drawings to be very effective in getting a point across and I became much better informed about the Old Testament myself.

I have written in the Introduction of *Economics for a Beautiful World* how I was affected by reading Hugh Schonfield's books *The Passover Plot, Those Incredible Christians,* and *The Politics of God.* [See Appendix 1] I did, at some point, join the Mondcivitan Republic, but I was unable to contribute in any useful way. It was a relief to see Jesus in the role of a human Messiah — not as part of a divine Trinity — which gave me the first clue of what was expected of me. I was to help spread that message. But how?

The 1980's were very tough financial times for small farmers. By now our six daughters were all in college or beyond and I opted to enroll in a local community college to become a registered nurse, just in case I would end up becoming the primary breadwinner. The program included some liberal arts credits and it was the first time I was required to do any type of writing. I not only did very well but I found that I enjoyed it.

It was also during this time that the U.S. invaded Iraq. I was devastated, naively thinking that popular protest against the Viet Nam War would ensure that the U.S. would never again go to war. As if to add insult to injury, I became aware of the U.S. bombing of water sanitation plants in Iraq leading to many unnecessary deaths of their most vulnerable citizens. At this point, I began my effort to better understand U.S. foreign and domestic policy. I wrote about this in the Introduction to *We Have a Choice: Let's Just Do It*. [See Appendix 2] What started out as material for a church discussion group, ended up being a vehicle to advocate for Schonfield's vision of a Servant Nation.

So how does Charles Eisenstein's book *Climate: A new Story* relate to Schonfield's vision of a Servant Nation? I see it as a practical guide to attaining the result that Schonfield desired which Eisenstein describes as *Interbeing* — a world of peace and justice and wholeness.

CHAPTER 1: A CRISIS OF BEING

The lost truth is that our addiction to fossil fuels is caused by an unmet need that can be described as Interbeing.

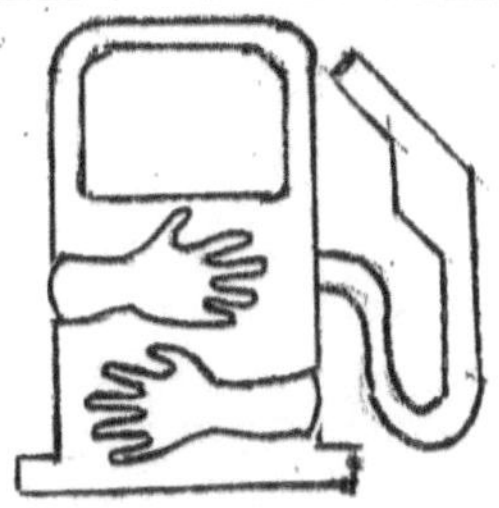

Who/what is responsible for this addiction?

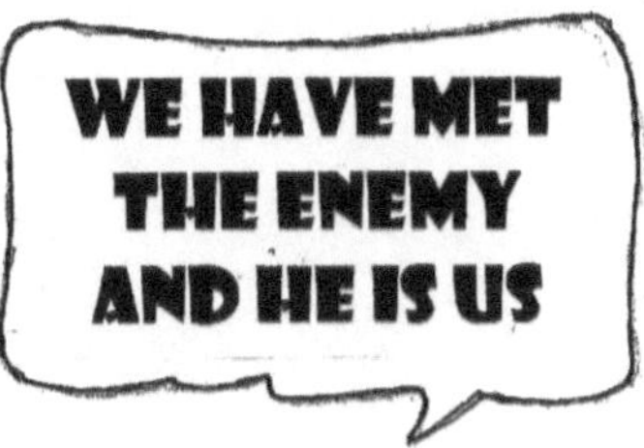

To solve the climate crisis and a Crisis of Being, we must give up our addiction to fighting.

ARMS EMBRACING A GAS PUMP

Our (the dominant culture's) addiction to fossil fuels. The addiction to fossil fuels, like all addictions, is caused by an unmet need. What is the unmet need behind the addiction to fossil fuels? What is it that we are really looking for in our quest for bigger, faster, and more? Basic human desires for connection, community, beauty, sacredness, and intimacy are met with faux substitutes that temporarily numb but ultimately heighten the longing. Ecological degradation is an inevitable consequence of the mythology of Separation that has dominated the last several centuries (and to an extant the last several millennia). The essence of the Story of Separation is the separate self in a world of other. Naturally then, we are in competition with each other. The same goes for humanity vis-à-vis nature. The more control we can exercise over the impersonal forces of nature, the better off we will be. Our destiny, then, is to ascend beyond nature's original limits, to become its lords and masters. The Story of Separation reverberates through every institution of the modern world. Every aspect of society, the economy and the political system must come into alignment with a new story — the story of *Interbeing*. The world is part of me, just as I am part of it. When we restore the internal ecosystem — the fullness of our capacity to feel and love — only then will there be hope of restoring the outer.

MESSAGE IN SPEECH BALLOON

We are the enemy. The ecological crisis is calling us to a

deeper kind of revolution. Its strategy involves restoring what the modern worldview and its institutions have rendered nearly extinct: our felt understanding of the living intelligence and connectedness of all things. So who are the enemies of the revolution and how do we identify them? "They", in fact, includes each one of us who participates in this civilization. Are you able to get into your car, knowing the effect of emissions and oil spills and the geopolitics of oil extraction? The point is that we are deluding ourselves. Our political discourse is rife with good-versus-evil narratives. It is obvious to each side that they are good and the other side is evil. Both sides agree on that. Both sides also agree on the strategic template for victory: arouse as much outrage and indignation as possible among the Good Folk so that they will rise up and cast down the Evil Folk. Those in our society typically misunderstand the causes of others' opinions and behaviors. To blame evil is to misdiagnose the problem. Focusing on the bad guys, we become blind to deeper, systemic causes, forever chasing false solutions that actually maintain the status quo.

CROSSED-OUT FIGHTERS

The addiction to fighting must be overcome. Fighting the enemy is futile when you inhabit a system that has the endless creation of enemies built into it. If that is to change, then one of the addictions — more fundamental than the addiction to fossil fuels — that we are going to have to give up is the addiction to fighting. The addiction to fighting draws from a perception of the world as composed of enemies. In a world of competitors, well-being comes through domination. In a world of random natural forces, well-being comes through control. War is the mentality of control in its most extreme form. Respect for nature is inseparable from respect for all beings, including the human. Climate change, therefore, calls us to a greater transformation than a mere change in our energy sources. It calls us to transform the fundamental relationship between self and other, including the relation between the collective self of humanity and its "other", nature. Our converging crises are initiating humanity into the new and ancient mythology of *Interbeing*.

CHAPTER 2: BEYOND CLIMATE FUNDAMENTALISM

Fundamentalism reduces a complex subject such as climate change to the simple. All must be sacrificed to one overarching goal – the reduction of CO_2 emissions…

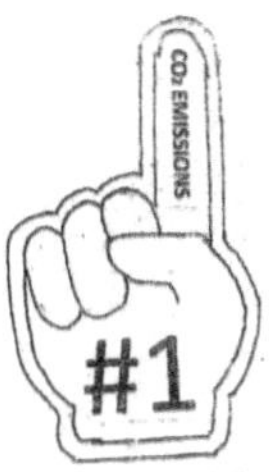

…thus, that priority must trump all other causes…

…thus ensuring that the *status quo* remains "set in stone".

NUMBER ONE FOAM HAND

The reduction of CO2 has become the defining goal of the climate change movement. It closely parallels the dynamics of two institutions of our civilization: money and war. Millions of people sacrifice time, energy, and family, and what they really care about in pursuit of money. Disciplined by an existential threat, a nation at war turns away from culture, leisure, civil liberties and everything that is of no utility to the war effort. The standard climate change narrative, which lends itself to the same focus on a universal cause and the same mentality of sacrifice to an all-important end, has alienated many working-class people and minorities from environmentalism because it carries a patronizing message of "We know better than you do what you should be caring about". It invalidates their grievances.

LARGE "X" ON SPEECH BALLOON OF CAUSES

The undermining of all other causes. If we want to foster a broad social consensus to protect and heal the planet, then we need to undo this logic at the source. The mind that is conditioned in Separation will protest, "But it is true! None of these things are relevant if the atmosphere warms by ten degrees". This belief depends on a world-story that does not recognize the intimate interconnectedness of all things. In *Interbeing*, we know that health for one natural system and health for the human family is impossible to sustain without health for all natural systems and all of humanity. If we want a healthy world, we need to understand that genocide and ecocide, human degradation and ecological degradation, are part of the same fabric, and that neither will change without the other changing. Earth is a complex living system whose homeostatic maintenance depends on the robust interaction of every living and nonliving subsystem.

We cannot expect a miserable, oppressed populace to exercise much care for anything outside its immediate survival and security. While the poor are kept in a state of survival anxiety through sheer deprivation, the rich suffer poverty of another kind: lack of community, connection, meaning, and intimacy, which can cause severe psychological stress even in conditions of material plenty. Herein lies a link between economic justice, social justice, and the environment. We will continue to abuse our fellow human beings, even our own Mother Earth, as long as we carry unhealed social traumas. This does not mean "heal our traumas first before we try to heal the environment". It is to recognize that social healing and ecological healing are the same work. Neither is to be privileged over the other; neither can succeed without the other. From the causal logic of *Interbeing*, it is easy to understand how a society that exploits and abuses its most vulnerable will also exploit and abuse nature.

STONE WITH WORDS "STATUS QUO"

The status quo is maintained. The term "social justice" may be too narrow to encompass the kinds of social healing that must happen for us to be able to fully enact our love for the planet. Traditional areas of social activism that aim to address racism, poverty, inequality, misogyny, and so forth are important but they leave unchallenged key institutions like education, medicine, money, and property often engaging them only in terms of equal application of existing systems, when the systems themselves are inherently oppressive whatever the race, gender, or sexual orientation of their subjects. Among the many causal narratives to apprehend climate change, or any other issue, our culture chooses the one that best preserves the status quo. The dominant culture adopts the narrative that sustains its dominance.

CHAPTER 3: THE CLIMATE SPECTRUM AND BEYOND

The roadmap to the climate spectrum ranges from skepticism to catastrophism…

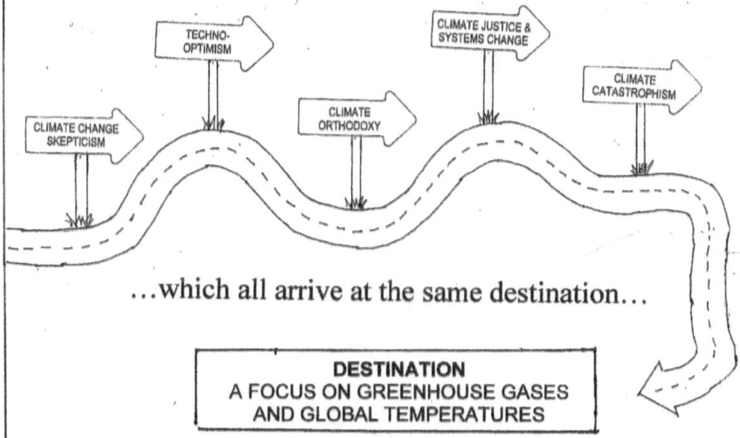

…which all arrive at the same destination…

…when the real problem is climate derangement.

ROADWAY AND SIGNS

The climate spectrum

1. Climate change skepticism.

Even modest departure from climate orthodoxy draw the epithet "denialism".

2. Techno-optimism

What is needed is simply to turn our focus to the problems, to incentivize their solutions, thereby uniting science and finance toward meeting humanity's newest challenge.

3. Climate orthodoxy

The burning of fossil fuels poses a grave threat to humanity and the planet. Therefore, we need to wean ourselves off fossil fuels as quickly as possible, transition to carbon-neutral energy technologies, and encourage economic policies of sustainable development and green growth.

4. Climate justice and systems change

This viewpoint says that climate change is inextricably linked to our economic system and various institutions of social oppression. Climate change isn't only an environmental issue, it is a social, racial, and economic issue. The system's dependency on the profits from a fossil-fuel-based industrial economy means that climate change can only be addressed by changing capitalism as we know it.

5. Climate catastrophism

This viewpoint basically says that it is already too late to prevent catastrophic climate change, except perhaps with an immediate response far beyond anything that is politically conceivable today and perhaps not even then.

DESTINATION SIGN

As with many polarizing issues, it is the hidden assumptions, shared by both sides and questioned by neither, that are most significant. The roadmap of the conventional spectrum of opinion on climate change includes positions that seem extreme and mutually opposed. They are not. However acutely opposed they may seem, hidden agreements unite them, and it is these hidden agreements that make the problem unsolvable. What could possibly unite such disparate viewpoints? They share a focus on greenhouse gases and global temperatures. On the one end of this spectrum, it is that they aren't a problem; on the other, that they spell the end of civilization. All agree with the general consensus that puts climate change and carbon at the heart of environmentalism. Accordingly, most of the skeptics throw out the baby of care for nature with the bathwater of the standard anthropogenic global warming (AGW) narrative. Similarly, alarmists unwittingly demote other environmental and social issues to secondary importance to their focus on AGW.

SHOUTING FIGURE WITH HAIR ON FIRE AND MESSAGE

We are engaged in the wrong debate. Neither "side" is right. Other issues are the hidden drivers of climate instability. Climate change is a symptom of ecosystem degradation, a process that goes back at least five thousand years and has reached peak intensity today. It arises from the basic relationship that has prevailed between civilization and nature. The main threat is not warming per se; it is what we might call "climate derangement". This derangement is caused primarily by the degradation of ecosystems worldwide: the draining of wetlands, the clear-cutting of forests, the tillage and erosion of soil, the decimation of fish, the destruction of habitats for development, the poisoning of air, soil, and water with chemicals, the damming of rivers, the extermination of predators, and so on leaving the ecosphere unable to cope with the additional greenhouse gases emitted through human activity. Climate change is inviting us to forge a different kind of relationship, one that holds the planet and all of its places, ecosystems, and species sacred – not only in our conception and philosophy, but in our material relationship. We must enact a civilization-wide unifying purpose that will restore beauty, health, and life to all that has suffered during the Ascent of Humanity.

CHAPTER 4: THE WATER PARADIGM

We should look at climate change through the lens of water rather than the lens of temperature and carbon because water is essential for life itself.

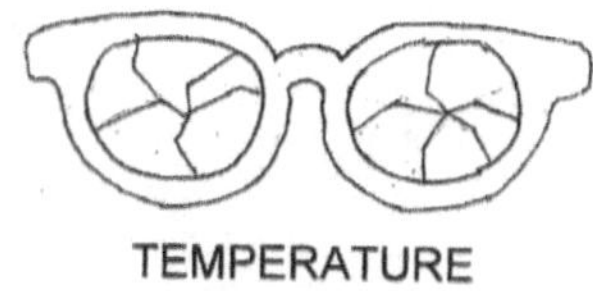

The water cycle depends on the health of the forests and other "organs" of the earth which are already severely deranged...

...resulting in the climate becoming drier over the last five thousand years.

TWO DIFFERENT LENSES

The clear lens represents water, while the cracked, distorted lens represents temperature and carbon. One thing that gets lost in the climate debate is that Earth's climate is already severely deranged. This is hard to see when the conversation is about global averages and the predictions of computer models. But severe climate change is already devastating the lives of millions of people. To see it, we have to look through a different lens – not temperature and carbon, but water. While most of the discourse around climate change focuses on temperature, water is the climatic factor that most directly impacts life. What we will see is that by putting water first, the carbon and warming problem will be solved as well. The paradigm shift when it comes to climate is not really from carbon to water; it is a shift from a geo-mechanical view to a Gaian view, a living systems view.

SAD EARTH HOLDING A DYING TREE

The fate of the forests and other "organs" of the earth. They are in steep decline. In a healthy water cycle, evaporated water from the ocean moves over the continents, where it falls as rain. A tiny fraction of that precipitation runs off directly, but most of it is absorbed by soil and vegetation, while some percolates into underground aquifers, eventually surfacing as springs that feed streams and rivers. Once the water is in the soil and water table, plants and especially trees steadily transpire it back into the air, providing a source of rain through the dry season. Depending on the region, some 30-90 percent of rainfall originates not directly from the ocean, but from evapotranspiration of water from soil and vegetation.

Deforestation, on the other hand, leads to soil erosion and the reduced capacity of the land to absorb water, and consequently worse flooding after heavy rains. Furthermore, without the deep roots of trees to bring moisture from deep underground and replenish atmospheric moisture, droughts tend to be longer and drier. This in turn puts greater stress on remaining forests, which become susceptible to fires and disease. When the rains do come, they run off the parched earth, taking the soil with them.

Virgin grasslands exercise many of the same functions that forests do, effectively soaking up rainfall and protecting soil, preventing flooding, ameliorating drought, seeding cloud formation, and building the water table. Wetlands, as the name suggests, are also crucial for a healthy water cycle. They slow the migration of water from land to sea, giving it time to soak down into aquifers and evaporate up into the atmosphere to be a source of rainfall. Owing to civil engineering projects such as the straightening of meandering rivers for navigation, as well as the near extinction of beavers, the slow process of water from land to sea was greatly hastened.

STRESSED, DRYING EARTH

The earth is dying. The Standard Narrative of climate

change contends that climate was relatively stable until the twentieth century, when industrial emissions started to become significant. Whether or not this is the case in terms of temperature, in terms of water the last few thousand years have seen dramatic changes in climate. As recently as Roman times, elegant cities stood in what is now desert, nourished by long-gone forested watersheds. The land is dying before our eyes, as it has been doing since ancient times. This is bigger than cutting greenhouse emissions. It is reversing a relationship to soil and sea that has been part of civilization for thousands of years.

CHAPTER 5: CARBON: THE ECOSYSTEMS VIEW

We should be focusing on "land use changes" (ecosystem destruction) as the cause of climate derangement…

…rather than focusing on fossil fuel emissions…

…and depending on technologies such as geoengineering…

…while relying on quantitative data to make decisions about climate change.

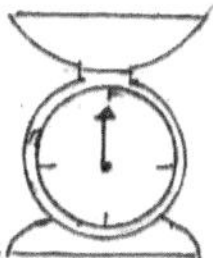

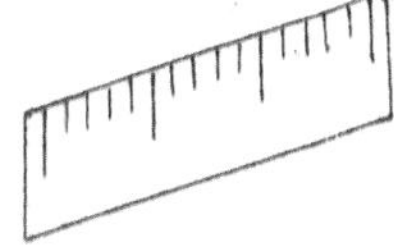

TRACTOR WITH PLOW AND LOGGING TRUCK

Agriculture and logging—examples of land use changes. Whether or not we reduce fossil fuel emissions, in the absence of ecological healing on every level, climate derangement will continue to worsen. To enter the ecosystem paradigm through the carbon lens, we must look at an item of the carbon budget that is much less certain than fossil fuel emissions—the release of carbon from "land use changes" (a euphemism for ecosystem destruction)—and, equally uncertain, the capacity of intact ecosystems to absorb and sequester carbon. Wetlands deposit more carbon in soil than any other ecosystem. Together with mangroves and salt marshes, wetlands account for half of biological carbon capture globally according to some estimates. Peatlands are another massive carbon sink—carbon that can enter the atmosphere when the peatlands are drained, deforested, or burned. Intact grasslands inhabited by herds of large herbivores have a tremendous capacity to sequester carbon in the soil. Sadly, 97 percent of the original North American high grass prairie has been converted to cropland, suburbs, and sown pasture. Today, most of this land is a carbon emitter, because it is cultivated for crops. As with wetlands and grasslands, destruction of forests turns land from a carbon sink to a carbon source. According to some estimates, the total number of trees on earth has fallen by nearly half since the dawn of civilization. Less recognized as a problem than deforestation is forest degradation, primarily a result of logging, insect damage, and forest fires.

CROSSED-OUT NERF HAND DECLARING CO² EMISSIONS ARE OUR NUMBER ONE CONCERN

Ecosystem disruption has turned many areas from carbon sinks into carbon sources. So why is there such an emphasis on fossil fuel emissions? First, and most simply, it is a lot easier to measure or estimate fossil fuel emissions than it is emissions from land use changes. In our present political culture, policymakers, treaty negotiators, and regulators need quantitative measures to define goals, agreements, and rules based on a "carbon budget". Likewise, biological carbon flows do not lend themselves easily to climate modeling compared to emissions. Last, the focus on emissions rests comfortably in the predominant geo-mechanical view of the planet, which sees Earth as a complicated machine rather than a living, complex organism. The point here is not that emissions don't matter. It is a call for a shift in priorities. On the policy level, we need to shift toward protecting and healing ecosystems on every level, especially the local. On a cultural level, we need to reintegrate human life with the rest of life, and bring ecological principles to bear on social healing. On the level of strategy and thought, we need to shift the narrative toward life, love, place, and participation.

TECHNOLOGY SYMBOL

Geoengineering as a solution. Many climate scientists conclude that the only practical solution is what is known as *geoengineering*—the artificial altering of the atmospheric composition and surface reflectivity of the planet in order to reduce global temperatures. These cooling measures will allow the real problem to continue unabated. Thinking we have solved the problem, we will be able to proceed with ecosystem destruction, covering up the symptom while worsening the disease.

SCALE AND RULER

Quantitative data leaves out the unmeasurable. In order to value what measurements and models leave out, we need another basis upon which to make our choices. It is the living planet paradigm, based on the Story of *Interbeing* that says that the health of all depends on the health of each.

CHAPTER 6: A BARGAIN WITH THE DEVIL

The shift of environmentalism from the love of nature to fear of human survival due to global climate change…

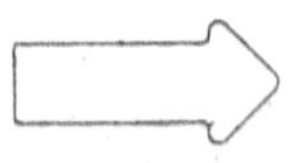

…is leaving ordinary people passive and giving even more power to the "powers that be" whose solutions consist of rewards (often to corporations) and punishments (which can easily be avoided) and cannot produce real care for nature, while their appeals to self-interest can only lead to more harm to the planet…

…but people are realizing that nature has rights, too.

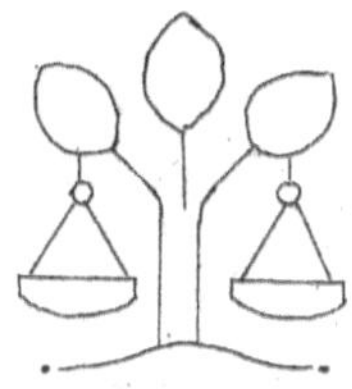

ARROW CONNECTING LOVE OF NATURE POSTER WITH SYMBOL OF GLOBAL CLIMATE CHANGE

The shift of emphasis of environmentalists. In adopting climate as their keystone narrative, environmentalists have made a bargain with the Devil. At first, climate change seemed a boon to environmentalism, a potent new argument for things environmentalists have always wanted, a new reason to shut down strip mines, to conserve the forests, and ultimately to end the expansion of a consumerist society. Finally, there was a do-or-die reason to implement agricultural practices that regenerate the soil; restore forests and wetlands; build smaller homes in higher density communities; implement economies of reuse; up-cycling and gift; foster bicycle culture; and spread home gardening. However, the premises of the environmental conversation shifted away from love of nature and toward fear for our survival. The movement moved from the heart to the mind, asking that we be motivated by distant consequences such as rising sea levels and other climate-related disasters.

FIGURE AT PODIUM

The "powers that be" — the wealthy nations of the Global North. Because the consequences of climate change are far off in time and space, people de-prioritize it in favor of more immediate issues. For most people, compared to their mortgage payment or their children's health, climate change seems quite remote and theoretical – something that is only happening in the future or on the news. The climate issue is usually presented in doom-and-gloom terms that make people feel powerless to do anything about it, while at the same time feeling guilty about their inaction and their complicity in the fossil fuel economy. This leads to various kinds of psychological denial to alleviate the guilt. So far the elite nations are able to insulate themselves from the harm that ecological destruction causes. Therefore it seems unreal. The air conditioner still runs. The car still goes. The credit card still works. The garbage truck takes away the trash. There is food in the supermarket and medicine in the pharmacy. The routines that define normal life are still intact. As long as normal routines continue, most people will not be persuaded to take meaningful action. The people become passive. The "powers-that-be" are quite comfortable with climate change when it is conceived in a way that gives more power to themselves. They are charged with the Promethean task of keeping the global industrial machine running at ever increasing speed, and safeguarding at the same time the biosphere of the planet. This will require a quantum leap in surveillance and regulation. These strategies call for more centralization, in particular, for a stronger state. Climate change portends a revolution in the relationship between nature and civilization, but that is not a revolution in the more efficient allocation of global resources in the program of endless growth. It is a revolution of love. It is to know the forests as sacred again, and the mangroves and the rivers, the mountains and the reefs, each and every one. We should understand that the revolution is to love all beings (including other humans) for themselves and not for their use. All expressions of the mindset of exploitation must change in tandem; each reflects and supports the rest. That is why all the revolutions under way today are the same revolution.

TREE WITH BALANCE SCALES

Symbol of the rights of nature. The growing Rights of Nature movement seeks to secure legal status for non-human beings; so far, Bolivia, Ecuador, and New Zealand have written these rights into law. This would elevate *interbeing* to something more than a personal philosophy or religious orientation. It would enshrine it as a fundamental principle of a different kind of society.

CHAPTER 7: THE REVOLUTION IS LOVE

In the Story of Separation, what happens to the biosphere needn't affect us…

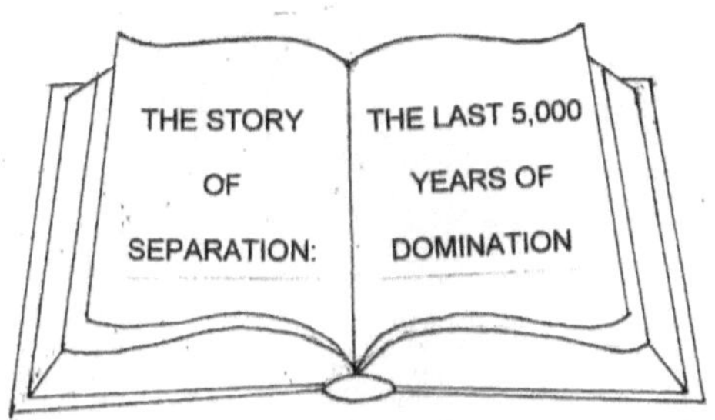

…except as a temporary, practical matter that we can solve with new technology to make us independent of nature, but which will continue the degradation of the planet…

…until we understand that the revolution is love - of the planet and all its beings.

BOOK

The Story of Separation. What is the Story of Separation? For the last 5,000-plus years we have lived in the same mythology: the story of a discrete and separate self in a desacralized world that is other. Love violates the Story of Separation. Love is the expansion of self to include another, whose well-being becomes part of one's own. The healing of our planet will not come without love for our planet. No one can logically persuade somebody to fall in love. We might be able to convince them to support one policy over another on utilitarian grounds, but engaging the planet as an instrument of our utility is what has gotten us into this mess to begin with. This is something that the entire spectrum of climate change positions, from skepticism to catastrophism, misses. A world in which we drain swamps and discharge toxic waste, in which animals are confined in feedlots, in which wealth concentrates in ever fewer hands, and in which people hate each other because of the color of their skin, is necessarily a world where the climate is spinning out of balance.

TECHNOLOGY SYMBOL

Our reliance on technology. Suppose that human ingenuity is unlimited, as is our capacity to replace ecosystem services with technological substitutes. While it is fashionable to attribute the collapse of past civilizations to ecological degradation, these narratives are subject to critique. History is often a projection screen for contemporary prejudices. In an era when we fear ecological collapse, it is natural that we would view history through that lens. Historical examples can also be used purposely to intensify the alarm that environmentalists hope will motivate change. However, the change we need must come from a different place than self-interested alarm. Maybe the significance of climate change is not "Change or perish", but an invitation to reorient civilization toward beauty rather than acquiring more stuff. Starkly confronting us with the results of our power, it asks, "What kind of world do you want to live in?" Whether or not endless technological adaptation to an ever-more-degraded ecosystem is actually possible, the *perception* that it is possible presents us with the necessity of making a conscious choice. If ecological degradation had the power to force us to choose a healing path, it would have happened already. Therefore, the choice to take the healing path will have to be made on some basis other than compulsion. It will not come through fear of personal or civilizational extinction.

HEART-SHAPED LEAVES

Love of our planet and all its beings. What do we choose from if we don't choose from fear of extinction? We can choose love. Modern people live almost entirely in a realm of products, media, and the indoors. One consequence of this is an ever-growing loneliness - an ache that nothing in the indoor world, manufactured world, or digital world can relieve. Surrounded by standardized commodities, visiting public spaces filled with strangers, interacting increasingly through the internet, and distanced from an intimate relationship with nature in a world of climate-controlled houses and packaged food, we are poor in our very existence. Why have we settled for a world that grows uglier and more degraded with each passing year? In order to reverse the course of ecocide, we may have to consciously choose a healing path. In order to choose it, we need to change the conditions from which we are choosing. To change these conditions, we need to implement a different economic system and understanding of nature, and more importantly, we need to recover our emphatic ability to feel. Therefore, the issue of environmental degradation and climate change cannot be separated from the need for social, economic and personal healing.

CHAPTER 8: REGENERATION

Regenerative Agriculture comprises an array of techniques that rebuild soil, water, and biodiversity. So why is it so marginal? There are several roadblocks in place.

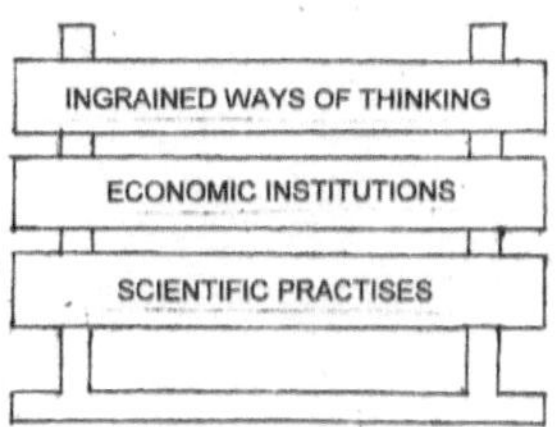

Industrial agriculture is not needed to feed a hungry world since small, local farms are more productive, therefore…

…governments should encourage the transition to Regenerative Agriculture, which leads to hydrological health as well…

…while we await the realization of human evolutionary purpose by observing positive indigenous practices and learning how to best restore the ecosystem to health.

ROADBLOCK

The determents to Regenerative Agriculture (RA). RA comprises an array of techniques that rebuild soil, water, and biodiversity. Typically, it uses cover crops and perennials so that bare soil is never exposed, fosters synergistic relationships among multiple food and non-food crops, restores the natural water cycle, and grazes animals in ways that mimic herd animals in nature. Whether from the carbon frame, the water frame, or the biodiversity frame, RA makes ecological sense. So why does it remain so marginal? The reason is its incompatibility with ingrained ways of thinking, economic institutions, and scientific practices. It is very difficult to isolate and quantify the effects of any single RA practice, thus it does not fit easily into current scientific protocol. Furthermore, the pesticide, fertilizer, and genetically modified seed companies that fund most agriculture research have little incentive to fund studies of practices that require none of the above.

CROSSED-OUT LARGE FARM IMPLEMENT

Industrial farming should be discontinued. It is unsustainable in the long term, and it doesn't even outperform ecological agriculture in the short term. Figuratively and literally, we need to go back to the land. Unfortunately, U. S. policy has encouraged the opposite, aggressively pushing the interests of large agribusinesses around the globe. For there to be meaningful healing on this planet, "impossibilities" like more people growing food cannot remain impossible.

This will take a wholesale civilizational transformation. It would require spending more time per capita on food production to feed ourselves and heal the land at the same time. It might require widespread home gardens, and government policies to encourage them. To align our society with ecological healing is not impractical. It just needs a shift in our perceptions, priorities, and laws.

MESSAGE ON PAPER

Governmental support for RA. Some kind of public subsidy is needed to support this transition. Since agriculture is already highly subsidized in many countries, that money could easily be transferred to RA. In the U.S., some 85 percent of farm subsidies go to the largest 15 percent of farm operations. As a general rule, what is good for the soil is good for water. Hydrological health is a happy side effect of soil health. Earth is demanding a transformation of our civilization's fundamental priorities. It is demanding we reorder our civilization and all its institutions accordingly. Money, government, law, and technology all must change.

GLOBE AND HUMAN HANDS

Our human evolutionary purpose. RA practices are rooted in a mindset and way of relating that goes back tens of thousands of years outside of civilization. It is a myth that hunter-gatherers were mere occupants of pristine "nature". Rather, their deliberate, sustained influence on their local territory allowed for sustainable harvest of plants over centuries and possibly thousands of years. Entire landscapes that appeared to the untrained eye of white settlers as wild were anything but. It is easy to see how the perception of idle natives living in "virgin" wilderness facilitated intrusion onto their territory. We have a lot to learn from indigenous people who sustainably tended and enriched the lands and waters they called home. But more importantly, we must adopt the mentality that gave birth to those methods. That mentality is the product of the worldview called *Interbeing*, a story that unites the diverse mythologies of indigenous peoples. It means forging intimate, respectful relationships with nature in its specific, local embodiment. That is our human evolutionary purpose.

CHAPTER 9: ENERGY, POPULATION, AND DEVELOPMENT

Both sides of the climate debate take for granted that it would benefit humanity to continue using a lot of energy.

However, we could shift to a mode of development different from the Western model of the last several centuries...

...and achieve abundance since it is a state of mind and a function of relationships.

The problem is not the size of the global population, but rather, the distribution of wealth and goods.

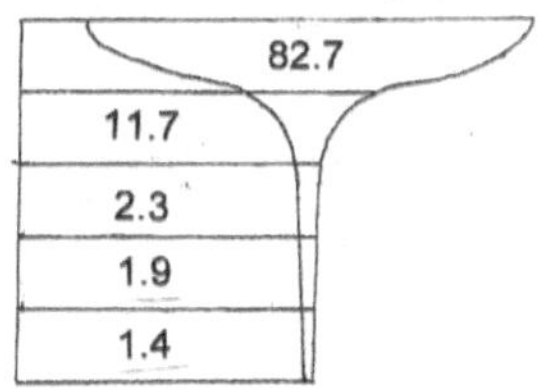

SPEECH BALLOONS OF OPPOSING SIDES OF THE CLIMATE DEBATE

Their positions on energy. The ecological crisis is supposed to be a wake-up call - not a challenge to overcome in order to stay on our current course. Both sides of the energy debate take for granted that it would benefit humanity to continue using a lot of energy (provided it can be done sustainably). In essence, it takes for granted the desirability and necessity of "progress" as we have known it, associating progress with a growing capacity to impose our will on the material world. Our profound impact on the planet owes itself to our harnessing of energy to do work.

CROSSED-OUT PICTURE ON THE STATE SEAL OF MINNESOTA

The Western worldview of progress. (The European immigrant claims the land of the Native American as he subdues the land). The energy crisis invites us into a less forceful way of life. We can shift to a mode of development different from the Western model of the last several centuries. Small towns and villages have emptied in a tide of urbanization propelled by the ideology and economics of development. Lost in the debate is the question of whether such an outcome is desirable. In the U. S., one in five people take psychiatric medication for depression and anxiety, suicide and addiction are at historic levels, one third of all children suffer abuse, and half of marriages end in divorce. These afflictions transcend race and class. Neither privilege nor success can protect against them. Public policy takes for granted people want more goods and services. There is a good explanation for this: Our economic system requires endless growth. Therefore, to choose from things that we really value such as family and community, we will need a radically different economic system.

THE CORNUCOPIA

An abundant life. Merely switching fuels will not alter the deep causes for human misery and the ecological devastation of the earth. Unless we turn toward other dimensions of ecological healing – soil, water, biodiversity, etc. – the condition of the biosphere will continue to worsen. And unless we address the roots of social and psychological misery, sustainable energy will just sustain more misery. Abundance is a state of mind and a function of social relationships. The conventional mind conceives abundance as a function of quantity, but in practice it depends equally on distribution and therefore on relationship. For example, food exists in theoretical superabundance on earth, yet it is so unequally distributed that nearly half goes to waste while one in five children goes hungry. The notion that human progress depends on *more and more* energy is obsolete. How we obtain energy and how we choose to use it will both be part of a larger choice: What kind of world shall we live in?

GLOBAL WEALTH DISTRIBUTION BY QUINTILES

The extreme disparity between the top one-fifth of the world population and the rest of the world. Global population is not the problem. The fixation on population obscures more fundamental issues. One of them is resource consumption. If everyone consumed resources at the rate of an average North American, the sustainable world population would be about 1.5 billion. Rather than talking about our own resource consumption, the industrialized nations would rather limit the reproduction of people "over there". Like the eugenics movement of the early twentieth century, the population control movement targets the world's most vulnerable people. By far the biggest population control efforts were those implemented outside the developed world, with the vigorous support of the United States government.

CHAPTER 10: MONEY AND DEBT

The global economy is like a rigged game of musical chairs
with some individuals, groups, and nations always left
standing, while others always get a chair.

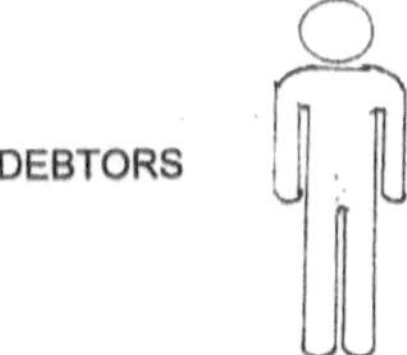

Our money system demands economic
growth in order for creditors to
collect the then larger debt created
by lending at interest. How is this
justified by economists?

The creditors are currently concen-
trating on the "development" of
the Global South, which means the
export of resources, causing an
environmental and social crisis.

An ecocidal economic system puts us
in a double bind, resulting in us
living as hypocrites. What can
be done about this dilemma?

STANDING AND SITTING FIGURES

The unfair dynamics of the global economy. The global economy is a system predicated from top to bottom on the maximization of self-interest, and therefore demanding we treat others as instruments of our own utility. Leftists love to blame corporations and their executives for the planet's predicament, but they are creatures of the system, carrying out structurally determined roles. Certainly there is some leeway for corporations to act more or less in the public interest, but to deviate too far from aggressive service to the bottom line faces the company with the iron law of the marketplace. They are the highly developed historical implement of the subordination of life and matter to the pursuit of self-interested value. Like so much of what we blame for our woes, they are more a symptom than a cause of the present crisis.

SPEECH BALLOON

The economic growth imperative. It is no accident that, because they take the current system as unchangeable, politicians left, right, and center all champion economic growth. They disagree about how to accomplish it, but everyone agrees that it is necessary. Economic growth is rarely questioned by any politician, since its premises are so deeply entrenched. However, numerous economists are arguing that we are nearing the limits of economic growth. Unfortunately, our present money system works only in the context of rapid growth. Without new money constantly being created, the means to service the debts is diminished, resulting in bankruptcies, unemployment, concentration of wealth, and the need for austerity to temporarily service the debts when rising income cannot.

EXPORT STAMP

The export of Global South resources. Development has happened over centuries in the West, where there is hardly anything we do in community anymore, and hardly anything that has not become a product or a service. Because there is so little left to convert into money, the system reaches to "less developed" parts of the world to maintain overall growth. Development loans finance the infrastructure to extract natural resources and haul them away, and to build industries to make local labor available to global corporations. In essence, growth is imported into the developed countries from the less developed. Furthermore, because their debt is at hopelessly high levels, the pressure to "develop" never ends. If ever the pace of resource extraction or labor market opening falters, then the creation of new financial wealth lags behind loan payments, and the country must cannibalize its existing wealth to pay creditors. That process is called "austerity".

DOCUMENT

A new money system. Why don't more people devote their lives to ecological or social healing? For many people, it is the necessity to make money in the very economy that is consuming the world's social and ecological capital. An ecocidal economic system puts us in a double bind: success in meeting one imperative (personal security) means failure in another (serving planet Earth), thus, resulting in a life of hypocrisy. So both greed and hypocrisy – the favorite targets of environmental righteousness – share a common root in our economic system. So how can we change it? The global debt regime is a core driver of environmental destruction; therefore, we need **Debt Cancellation.** An interest-based system is profoundly unecological; therefore we need **Negative-Interest Money.** The public should not bear the costs of polluting industries; therefore, we need the **Internalization of Ecological Costs.** The commons should be restored to public ownership; therefore we need a **Universal Basic Income.**

CHAPTER 11: AN AFFAIR OF THE HEART

If money is the keystone of the arch of modern society, the foundation is surely science, but the scientific world has not yet accepted that all matter is sentient.

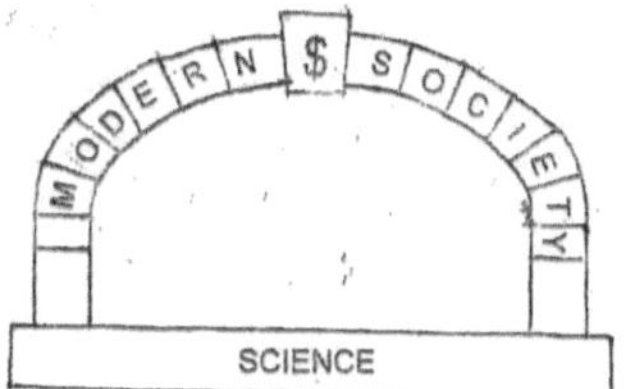

We have been warned that we are killing the planet, but we lack the humility to hear. However, we are facing repeated humiliation as our cultural mythology falls apart.

"From the Heart of the World"
&
"Aluna"

A mechanistic view of nature-as-thing numbs our compassion, facilitates our plunder, cripples our ability to serve as agents of positive transformation, and leaves us without allies.

Nature provides us with resources to be used for human benefit

NATURE-AS-THING MENTALITY

The reanimation of our world is crucial to ecological healing. If we live in the perception that the world is dead, we will inevitably kill what is alive.

God is in all things and nothing is not God

ARCH AND SPEECH BALLOON MESSAGE

The supporting structure of modern society and its rationale. If climate change indeed faces us with an initiation into a new phase of human civilization, then we might expect that science, like money, will undergo a profound change. Since our culture sees science as its foremost means to discover truth, to reject what science says seems the epitome of irrationality, tantamount to a willful denial of truth itself. Science in our culture is more than a system of knowledge production or a method of inquiry. So deeply embedded it is in our understanding of what is real and how the world works, that we might call it the religion of our civilization. It isn't a revolt against truth that we are seeing: it is a crisis in our civilization's primary religion. The spiritual essence of the religion of science is the opposite of its institutional arrogance: the Scientific Method embodies a deep and beautiful humility. It says, "I do not know, so I shall ask". Therefore we should not discard science but expand it to include what it has ignored and understand how it has been misused. Both the metaphysical assumptions of science and its institutional expression are part and parcel of the system that has laid waste to the world. We are on shaky ground indeed if we are to rely on trust in the institution of science, and by extension trust in authority generally, to deliver us from climate catastrophe.

DOCUMENTARIES

The message from our "older brother". Many indigenous people see a great peril coming upon us. There is a belief widespread among indigenous people that human activity, including ritual activity, is part of the glue that holds the world together. When we forget our proper function and cease to serve life, the world falls apart. The Sierra Nevada tribes of Columbia are famous today thanks to two films, *From the Heart of the World* and *Aluna*. Their elders tell us, "You mutilate the world because you don't remember the Great Mother. If you don't stop, the world will die". Why hasn't "little brother" (us) listened? Perhaps we have not listened because we have not yet come to humility. As our cultural mythology falls apart, we face repeated humiliation in the failure of our cherished systems of technology, politics, law, medicine, education, and more. Only with increasingly strenuous and willful ignorance can we deny that the grand project of civilization has reached a dead end.

NATURE-AS-THING SPEECH BALLOON MESSAGE

Humanity is separate from nature. This mentality sees nature primarily as a means to benefit humanity through its abundant "resources". Because of this we cannot fully understand the needs of land, ocean, soil, water, or forest. They become invisible to us through the lens of instrumental utilitarianism, through the lens of resources, minerals, commodities, and profit. Older cultures commonly believed that mountains, rivers, animal species, the ancestors, and other seen and unseen beings participated in human affairs and could alter the course of history. If the powers of nature are so great, then why haven't they put an end to the destruction we have wrought? It is because theirs is not a power of force against force. In that story, the deeper sponsoring assumption is if anything purposeful is to happen, we have to *make* it happen. It has no room for the agency of other beings to engineer synchronicity. We need to realize that "something" is listening.

MESSAGE IN HEART

We are not alone. The "something" that is listening is everything: earth, sky, water, air rocks, trees, animals, plants, along with beings we do not see and that have no name. God is in all things and nothing is not God. Truly, this is an affair of the heart.

CHAPTER 12: BRIDGE TO A LIVING WORLD

It is crucial that we bridge the huge gap between the dominant practices, policies, and perceptions and their solutions...

DOMINANT PRACTICES, POLICIES, AND PERCEPTIONS

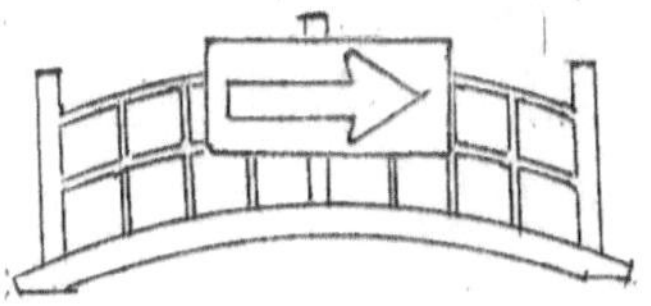

SOLUTIONS

...if we are to change course and move toward a living world by adopting these necessary policies and changes...

...especially turning away from pesticides...

... and demilitarizing society.

BRIDGE AND DIRECTIONAL ARROW

Where we are at and where we must go. How do we arrive at real solutions to the dominant practices, policies, and perceptions we now employ?

TO DO LIST

A partial list of the things necessary to reach our goal of a living world.

1. Promote land regeneration by connecting young farmers to land, helping farmers to transition to regenerative practices, and shifting agricultural subsidies away from conventional crops.

2. Institute a global moratorium on logging, mining, and drilling and develop all remaining primary forests, wetlands, and other ecosystems.

3. Expand the land protected in wildlife reserves and other reserves.

4. Establish new ocean reserves and expand existing ones.

5. Establish strict bans on driftnets and bottom trawling.

6. Ban disposable plastic bags for retail purchases. Phase out plastic beverage containers in favor of a refillable bottle infrastructure.

7. Reconstitute the World Bank to serve ecological healing rather than development.

8. Promote afforestation and reforestation projects globally with ecologically appropriate species.

9. Establish an "eco-corps" to address youth unemployment.

10. Change building codes, sanitation codes, and zoning laws to allow higher density development, tiny homes, composting toilets, aquaculture wastewater treatment, etc. Nullify all land use covenants that prohibit vegetable gardens.

11. Reintroduce and protect keystone species.

12. Carry out water restoration projects worldwide.

13. Localize the food system and promote economic localization generally.

14. Institute a negative-interest financial system through international agreement.

15. Apply pollution taxes.

16. Impose a deposit system for most manufactured goods.

LARGE "X" ON PESTICIDE CONTAINER

17. Turn away from pesticides. From Europe to Aus-

tralia to the Americas, insect biomass is in precipitous decline, a phenomenon that many scientists attribute to the growing use of insecticides over the past eighty years. To transition away from pesticides entails the wholesale deindustrialization of agriculture, in particular the ending of mono-cropping. Aside from forest and wetlands destruction, pesticides might be the most urgent environmental issue we face.

LARGE "X" ON MILITARY-INDUSTRIAL COMPLEX

18. Demilitarize society. What overarching aim does the military serve? Traditionally it was the interests of the nation-state; today it might be more the interests of transnational capital. On a deeper level, it serves the paradigm of domination through force. Demilitarization is therefore a necessary marker and sign of a civilizational shift of priorities. The environmental crisis invites us to change our priorities and put earth healing first, make ecological-social healing the primary conditioning parameter on every political decision. The military mind puts defeat of an enemy instead. More tangibly, the military sucks up prodigious amounts of energy, materials, money, and human talent. We are not going to see real earth healing while maintaining the military-industrial complex. If we want to live in a more beautiful world, we will have to give up central aspects of business-as-usual. What could be more starkly relevant a first step than demili-

tarization?

AFTERWORD

I recently read a small book by Naomi Klein entitled *The Battle for Paradise* with "paradise" being Puerto Rico. The "battle" was described in the Foreword of the book (written by members of the Professors Self-Assembled in Solidarity Resistance (PAReS)), as *"being waged between these opposing visions. On the one side lies the utopia (for us, a dystopia) of Puerto Rico as a resort for the wealthy. On the other, a utopian vision of a Puerto Rico that is equitable, democratic, and sustainable for all.*[1]

In the aftermath of Hurricane Maria (September, 2017), Klein, well known for her focus on the application of a "shock doctrine" of neoliberal policies following natural disasters, had accepted an invitation by PAReS in January, 2018 to speak about her work and to spend a week observing the resistance and responses of ordinary Puerto Ricans against the forces of disaster capitalism.

There are some things that remind me of the "to do list" that Charles Eisenstein is advocating to put us on the right path to a more beautiful world. **Local energy.** Klein met a biologist in a small mountain village who had understood the need for renewable energy and had installed solar panels on a community center twenty years previously. After Maria hit the island, it was the only source of energy for miles around. It should be noted that 98% of Puerto Rico's electricity is

---

1   Klein, Naomi (2018) *Battle For Paradise: Puerto Rico Takes on the Disaster Capitalists*, p. X, Haymarket Books

produced from imported fossil fuels. **Agro-ecological farming.** Klein met a trained agronomist in charge of a farm connected to a middle school where she teaches the students the practical skills of agro-ecology which is a term that refers to traditional farming methods that promote resilience and biodiversity, reject pesticides and other toxins, and commit to building social relationships between farmers and local communities. Again, it should be noted that roughly 85% of the food eaten by Puerto Ricans is imported. The people learned that they can do for themselves, in a democratic and community-building way, what the government fails to do.

However, compared to the forces of global capitalism, these commendable efforts seem like a "drop in the bucket", if even that. Klein notes that a government plan is already afloat to penalize communities that set up their own renewable energy micro-grids and the privatization of the educational system would surely eliminate agro-ecological farm schools. But as the legitimacy of our current system erodes, let's be prepared to promote a more beautiful world, starting with Eisenstein's list of recommendations.

About the Mondcivitan Movement

REBUILDING A *HOLYSTIC*[2] SERVANT NATION OF MANKIND

Mondcivitania is a virtual servant nation composed of all those who are willing to try and live by its principles which are based on love for our fellow human beings.

Being a holy nation has nothing to do with church membership or religious affiliation, nor with personal salvation and an afterlife. Our bond is the shared realization that all of life on this planet is a unity and that we are meant to live in love and community with everyone. We are by no means perfect, or can ever hope to be, but by following the Principles below, we can serve as an example to the rest of humanity that a beautiful world is possible. We don't need the rule of law which always protects the elite sector, but rather, the law of love which gives meaning and purpose to everyone. As we are a people, there is no formal membership—you are already a Mondcivitan if you find it right to live by these principles:

1. No-one is an Enemy

Mondcivitans acknowledge none as enemies, no mat-

---

2   With the spelling "holystic" the intention is to emphasize the idea of a "holy" Servant Nation (in other words—set apart for a special purpose, to be an exemplary people qualified to mediate on the behalf of mankind). It also includes the idea of holistic—the whole is greater than the sum of the parts.

ter what they may do; for to admit the existence of an enemy is to create a barrier, darkening understanding, breeding hatred, and giving encouragement and licence to cruelty and inhumanity.

2. No-one is a Foreigner

Mondcivitans recognize none as foreigners, or of a lower dignity, since all belong to the same human race. There shall be identical treatment of those outside of Mondcivitania as of those within it, treatment that is founded on reverence for the human personality.

3. Service to All

Mondcivitans shall ever promote and actively assist measures for the welfare and equitable unification of mankind, and shall at all times respond to the extent of its ability to calls for aid in emergency or catastrophe.

4. Complete Impartiality

Neither Mondcivitania, nor any of its citizens, shall under any circumstances engage in war or in preparation for war, or in aggression, oppression, or wilful misrepresentation. Mondcivitania shall ever hold itself free from all alliances, agreements and contractual obligations, whether open or secret, which can have the effect of favoring any group, party, section, or state, or any interests whatever, to the hurt or detriment of any others.

5. Work for Peace

Mondcivitans shall study to be impartial in all their relations and judgments, and shall labour in the cause of mediation and reconciliation.

6. True Democracy

The character of Mondcivitania is democratic and co-operative, based on mutual service and respect, holding all people in honor in public and private.

7. Equity and Justice

In its government and internal economy Mondcivitania shall continually seek to cultivate and display those standards of conduct which are equitable and just.

We do have a choice however and we can start to try to live by these principles in our personal lives. It is time for all those who ascribe to them to stand up and be counted as a citizen of this people in service to mankind. So all your comments and reports of activities to further these principles are welcome.

Mondcivitania is the successor to the Mondcivitan Republic (Commonwealth of World Citizens) legally constituted in 1956 and the International Arbitration League founded by Nobel Peace Prize Winner (1903) Sir William Randal Cremer.

Please join us at

www.mondcivitan.org

https://www.facebook.com/groups/mondcivitania

More information is also available at:

https://en.wikipedia.org/wiki/Mondcivitan_Republic

http://www.schonfield.org/

Appendix 1
Economics for a Beautiful World

INTRODUCTION

I spent much of my adult life trying to understand the true nature of U.S. foreign and domestic policy. In my book, *We Have a Choice: Let's Just Do It*, the conclusion I eventually arrived at can be summarized in the words of Rahul Mahajan from his book *The New Crusade: America's War on Terrorism:*

> *There can be no mistake about it — the United States is an empire, the most powerful in history... Empires are always about extraction of wealth from the provinces for the benefit of the center, without regard for the subject people. They may not benefit all social strata in the imperial nation — in fact, some of the lower classes have to fight and die to maintain the empire — but they always do benefit an elite. In most cases, the wealth is spread around, both among some broad strata of the imperial center, and among a native elite in the provinces, in both cases to help*
>
> *preserve political stability.*[3]

I wrote that book with the express purpose of exposing the writings of author Dr. Hugh J. Schonfield to a larger audience. I had, over a period of time, come to accept

---

3   Mahajan, Rahul 2002, p. 101-103, *The New Crusade: America's War on Terrorism,* Monthly Review Press, New York.

the main thesis of his book, The Politics of God[4]—that a divine plan was in progress to establish a Servant Nation that would act as the catalyst to bring peace and justice to the world. The response was negligible, until I shared a copy of the book with Stephen A. Engelking who offered to publish it. Although Schonfield was instrumental in establishing the nation he had envisioned, the world was not ready for it, so the fulfillment of the plan remains to be realized.

And then, Charles Eisenstein's book Sacred Economics came into my life. It was the "missing link" between Schonfield's vision and the practical means of carrying it out. I fervently believe we will see—as Eisenstein describes it—"the more beautiful world our hearts tell us is possible."

---

4   See the relevant section in this book.

Appendix 2
We Have a Choice

INTRODUCTION

June, 2019

These lessons represent my personal long-term process of trying to understand the true nature of U.S. foreign and domestic policy. This quest included enrolling in seven college classes—one at Metro State University taught by local peace activist, Jack Nelson-Pallmeyer, and six at the University of St. Thomas in their Justice and Peace Studies program under the direction of Rev. David Smith. I also gleaned much valuable information from library books, from Pacifica Radio's *Democracy Now!* and from various other alternative media.

I wrote the original version of these lessons for use in a discussion group in my home congregation, Christiania Lutheran Church, Lakeville, MN. Our church had hosted a visiting pastor, Benito Madembo, from the Iringa Diocese in Tanzania for a period of three weeks. For most of us, it was our first contact with a person from the Global South. We were impressed with his graciousness and beauty of spirit, but were troubled by the poverty that he and the majority of people in his homeland experienced. One of our responses was to initiate a study group seeking to understand why poverty persists in the Global South. I volunteered to lead the group, feeling it would give me an opportunity to synthesize and organize the information I had gathered from my six years of study.

I joined the Alliance for Democracy (AfD-MN) in 2000. The main emphasis of this group (no longer active) was to understand and expose the abuse of corporate power. We decided to use the lessons as part of our educational outreach. Discussion Questions, an introductory essay, and input from other AfD-MN members were added at this time.

I have long been interested in the concept of a prototype community which could model a sustainable society based on cooperation and equality that could serve as an example and incentive to all of mankind. I hope that this booklet can make a contribution to that end.

Highlighted below are two general themes that occur throughout the lessons.

1. The paradigm of the United States as a benevolent superpower is a myth.

U.S. PARADIGM

The United States is a benevolent superpower. It is our obligation, and therefore our earnest desire, to ensure peace, prosperity, freedom, and democracy, not only for U.S. citizens, but for all of humanity.

I realized during the first Gulf War (1991) that I could no longer reconcile U.S. foreign policy with the paradigm of U.S. as benevolent superpower. As U.S. citizens, we want to believe in the U.S. paradigm of benevolent superpower. We want to believe that our material wealth and our national greatness are the direct result of the form of government we instituted, the type of economic system we have developed, and the religious foundation on which our nation is built. We want to believe that we are a benevolent and caring people, that we value honesty and fairness, and that we reward initiative and hard work. Most of the people I know share these beliefs. I had accepted, without question, the paradigm of U.S. as benevolent superpower for over forty years. When that belief was shattered during the first Gulf War, I had to ask myself, **"If not benevolence, then what is the reality of U.S. foreign policy?"** The conclusion that I eventually arrived at can be summarized in the words of Rahul Mahajan from his book *The New Crusade: America's War on Terrorism*.

U.S. REALITY

There can be no mistake about it — the United States is an empire, the most powerful in history. Empires are always about extraction of wealth from the provinces for the benefit of the center, without regard for the subject people. They may not benefit all social strata in the imperial nation — in fact, some of the lower classes have to fight and die to maintain the empire — but they always do benefit an elite. In most cases, the wealth is spread around, both among some broad strata of the imperial center, and among a native elite in the provinces, in both cases to help preserve political stability.

If the U.S. ruling class is, indeed, harboring imperial

ambitions, at great cost to human rights, democratic ideals, and the natural environment, why do so many U.S. citizens continue to accept the U.S. paradigm of benevolent superpower at face value? Former AfD—MN member, David Shove, suggested the reason why the myth persists: *The myth of U.S. benevolence is the central ideological defense of the ruling class, ingrained in us by endless repetition until it seems "common sense," and thus an effective barrier to conflicting reports.* Imperialist powers seek to justify their position of dominance. The U.S. as benevolent superpower is the latest manifestation of 500 years of Western imperialism which has arrogantly proclaimed that it must shoulder "the white man's burden".

But is there more to this imperial mindset than just ruling class deception for the purpose of attaining/maintaining wealth and power? It would seem so. Former AfD-MN member, Betsy Barnum, in a Common Dreams article stated: *The United States has had, as a society, a sense of being "special" ever since people began coming to these shores looking for a place to practice their religion without oppression. The sense of America being a "promised land" has created a way of thinking about this nation that extends far beyond religious definitions. Since World War I, and especially since World War II, this sense of specialness has focused on American democracy as the highest form of democracy, something we are taught to believe it is our duty and our purpose to teach to other nations. We also view our way of life as the highest form of society and culture yet developed, characterized by individual freedom and affluence, and it is also something we believe is to be shared with the rest of the world.* The negative effects of

U.S. imperialism can be easily overlooked — both by the policy-makers and the citizenry — because of this over-riding internalization of specialness.

2. The biases inherent in the Western worldview of progress are devastating human solidarity and the natural environment.

Much will be said about the Western worldview of progress in the lessons, but noted here will be the nega-tive effect its inherent biases have had, and are continu-ing to have, on indigenous populations and the natural environment. The state seal of Minnesota[5] and a poem it inspired are revealing examples of these practically unconscious biases.

Give way, give way, young war-rior,
Thou and thy steed give way -
Rest not, though lingers on the hills
The red sun's parting ray
The rock bluff and prairie land
The white man claims them now,
The symbols of his course are here,
The rifle, ax and plough.

- Mary Eastman

The white European immigrant in the foreground lays claim to the land of the Native American who must therefore "give way". Why? The white man's course — progress — is regarded as superior to that of the Native American who, in fact, stands in the way of progress.

---

5   https://mnflag.tripod.com/1983seal.gif

The assumption is that progress will make life better. But for whom? Certainly not for the former inhabitants of the land. The gap between "developed" people and "underdeveloped" people widens and human solidarity is devastated.

The white man's symbols of progress—the rifle, ax and plough—indicate a consciousness that nonhuman life forms only have value through their use by humans. Animals are for food or sport. Nature is seen as an obstacle to be overcome and a resource to be exploited. Using the tools of modern science and technology in the quest for human benefit and financial gain, progress is accomplished by exploiting the living and nonliving resources of the planet. In the process, the natural environment is devastated.

My motivation in writing these lessons has been my belief that the human race is capable of being so much more than the current world situation would lead us to believe. Nelson Mandela, in his autobiography *Long Walk to Freedom*, expressed this thought: I know as well as I know anything that the oppressor must be liberated just as surely as the oppressed. The ruling elite in their desperate and misguided attempt to retain their privilege and wealth have deprived themselves of something of far greater value—the realization that individual human fulfillment can only be found in attaining a oneness with all of humanity, indeed, in attaining a oneness with all of creation as we live in harmony with each other and our natural environment.

Appendix 3
Guidelines for Study Circles

An optimum group size is six to eight members.

The group should decide on a convenient time and place to meet, frequency of meetings, length of time for the meeting, and who will facilitate.

It is important that each member read the assigned lesson prior to the group meeting. Write down questions or points you would like to discuss or call attention to. Feel free to discuss questions suggested by the group.

It is recommended, but not essential, that the role of facilitator rotate among the group members. What is important is that the facilitator not be looked on as the "teacher" or "expert". His/her duties include:

- making sure that the discussion remains focused. This often requires a delicate balance — don't force the group to stick to the question at hand, but don't allow the discussion to drift too far afield.

- making sure that each person has a chance to speak. Don't allow one or two people to monopolize the discussion. If necessary, decide on a time limit per person and appoint a timekeeper. Sometimes it is necessary to ask the quieter members of the group if they have anything to add.

If more than one person wishes to speak at the same time you may want to use a "stacking" procedure. A person is designated to recognize and list in order those who wish to speak. This can be done by members simply raising their hand. Then the speakers are called on in the order listed. Points of clarification are usually allowed outside of the list order. For example, if someone does not hear or does not understand the meaning of a word used, they can ask for clarification.

Opposing viewpoints are to be expected. Respect the opinions of others.